"In an increasingly complex world for parents and kids, Eliza provides much-needed counsel that is spiritually encouraging, easily accessible, and wonderfully practical."
– Joshua Cooley, *New York Times* bestselling author and long-time Kids Minister

"This book is jam-packed with wisdom that is biblically based, developmentally appropriate, and psychologically sound! Eliza offers excellent practical tips on how to respond to our kids' hearts with grace that will certainly cultivate emotional health, both in parents and kids alike!"
– Melinda C Capaldi, PsyD, clinical psychologist, Insight Care

"This resource is very assessible and highly practical! Being a parent of two young kids, I've found myself coming back to this amazing resource over and over and plan to keep doing so as my children continue to grow. I highly recommend it to any parent desiring to invest well in their children's emotional and spiritual health."
– Nathan Reed, Pastor of McLean Bible Church Tysons

"There is no manual on parenting. We are told 'congratulations!' and 'good luck' and then are left to figure it out on our own. Eliza Huie's book *Raising Emotionally Healthy Kids* is the closest thing we have to a manual! It is insightful, practical, and engaging and will provide you with the essential tools to equip your children. A must read!"

– **Dr. Mark Mayfield, author of** *Help! My Teen is Self-Injuring: A Crisis Manual for Parents* **and** *The Path Out of Loneliness: Finding and Fostering Connection to God, Ourselves, and One Another*

RAISING
Emotionally
Healthy
KIDS

RAISING

Emotionally
Healthy

KIDS

Help for Parents

ELIZA HUIE

10 Publishing
a division of 10ofthose.com

Copyright © 2022 by Eliza Huie

First published in Great Britain in 2022

British Library Cataloguing in Publication Data
A record for this book is available from the British Library

ISBN: 978-1-914966-13-2

Designed by Jude May

Printed in Denmark by Nørhaven
Cover images © eichinger julien, iStock

10Publishing, a division of 10ofthose.com
Unit C, Tomlinson Road, Leyland, PR25 2DY, England
Email: info@10ofthose.com
Website: www.10ofthose.com

To my children.
(3 John 1:4)

Contents

Series introduction

Raising kids is a daunting endeavor for even the most skilled parents. The challenge is compounded by the high-tempo lives we live. Between work, school, practices, recitals, games, youth group, performances, time with friends, and the myriad of other things demanding our time, parenting feels more like a logistical nightmare than a divine call to shape the lives of our children.

We have partnered with 10Publishing to produce the Raising Kids series. These resources have been written to bring welcome help to parents who may be feeling overwhelmed by the many challenges parenting brings. The series contains short books on vital issues parents face in today's day and age, as well as issues parents of every generation wrestle with. Issues like a self-made identity, sex, gender fluidity, our results-driven culture, grace-centered parenting, technology, and social media are all covered in these books. The authors write from a deep understanding of God's Word coupled with their own experience of raising kids, making each book rich with practical and personal wisdom that is sure to benefit any parent.

These short, easy-to-read books do not attempt to be exhaustive manuals on any one of the topics. Instead, they offer strategic insights that are timeless and immediately applicable. The goal is not to fully outfit you for an expedition over Everest but to give you a few secure handholds and footholds that will help you hang on and advance up the mountain of raising kids.

The world in which children are growing up is full of uncertainties and challenges. As parents, it can be hard to know how to help them manage their own emotions, and keep hold of hope and truth. In *Raising Emotionally Healthy Kids*, Eliza Huie explains how parents can give their children grace-filled responses that will point to God's faithfulness in all the emotional ups and downs of life.

Curtis W. Solomon
Director, The Biblical Counseling Coalition

Why read this book?

Numbers provide perspective. When it comes to children and emotional health, the numbers are concerning. Research indicates that nearly one in three adolescents will meet the criteria for an anxiety disorder by the age of eighteen.[1] Other studies reveal that one in six children between the ages of six and seventeen have already been diagnosed with a mental illness.[2] Pew Research reported that the number of teenagers who experienced depression increased by 59% over a ten-year period.[3] New studies will soon reveal more about the emotional impact of bullying, social media, and excessive exposure to traumatizing news and images, as well as the effects living through the global pandemic of 2020 has had on children's mental health. There has been an alarming increase in suicide among children and teens, and growing diagnoses of mental health disorders are being assigned to kids at earlier ages. All this confirms to parents that there are good reasons to be concerned about their child's mental and emotional health.

But numbers may not be the motivating factor in your desire to learn how to raise emotionally healthy kids. Perhaps your own struggle with emotional health is compelling you to be attentive to your child's emotional state. Or maybe you just want to do all you can to help your kids develop well in all areas of their life, which includes their mental well-being.

As a counselor, I get asked many questions about kids and mental health. The ones listed below are just a sampling of those asked by parents wanting to help their children as they grow up in a world plagued with emotional distress. Maybe you have asked some of these questions or ones like them.

"What are the signs of depression in children?"
"When should I be concerned about my child's emotional health?"
"How do I help a suicidal teen?"
"What are some healthy ways to help kids navigate the emotional challenges they face today?"

"How do I get my teenage son to open up and talk to me?"

"Can you recommend resources for an elementary-aged girl who hates her body?"

"At what age should I consider counseling for my child? Is there an age that is too young?"

"How do I know if my child is struggling with mental health or if this is just a phase of teenage angst?"

"Does my child need to be on medication for their emotional struggles?"

Children today face emotional struggles at earlier ages and at deeper levels than any other generation. Many of the struggles they commonly face were not issues when their parents were growing up. While their parents did experience emotional challenges as kids, anxiety, depression, addiction, identity struggles, and general mental health issues were problems of adulthood not childhood.

The numbers mentioned above and the struggles kids face today have left parents deeply concerned for their child's emotional health. The prevalence of how often these questions, and many like them, are asked reveals parents' acute need for direction. Parents are desperate to know what they can do to raise emotionally healthy children. If you find yourself asking questions like the ones above, you are not alone. If you are a parent who desires to raise up emotionally healthy children, this book is for you. If you are a parent in the midst of walking with a struggling child, I pray you find help in these pages.

What follows are five helpful tips to guide you as you parent through the ups and downs of emotions. Each chapter offers practical help on how to nurture the emotional health of children. You will gain an understanding of what promotes emotional health and learn signs that indicate your child may be struggling. The tips, though brief, provide direction on how to engage with the emotional struggles children face, and how to offer help and lasting hope anchored to the enduring promises of God.

This book is not a formula. As much as I would love to offer you a few simple steps toward a solution that would ensure your child never has to deal with emotional or mental health struggles, children are unique individuals. We must love them as people, not solve them as problems. What I will offer is counsel to foster emotional health in your child and also in you.

The tips I share are offered from my experience

as a biblical counselor, as a clinical mental health professional, and as a parent. My husband and I raised three children, and I share some advice taken from our successes as well as our failures. We are not perfect parents. I am not a faultless counselor. But God has given us incredible grace in all we faced, and that same grace is available to you. We all need the Lord's help in raising our children. We all need prayer as we parent. As you start this book, know that I have prayed for you. As you begin, this is my prayer for all the parents who read this book:

Dear God,
Care for the parents who have picked up this book.
When they are afraid, bring courage; when they are
hurting, provide comfort; when they are discouraged,
give hope. Remind them that as much as they love
their child, your love for their child is infinitely greater.
You have specifically chosen them to parent this child,
and you will equip them for all that they face. Remind
them that nothing is outside of your control and care.
Guide them as they seek to attend to the emotional
well-being of their children, and help them to be
conduits of your love and grace to their children.
In Jesus' name, amen.

TIP 1

Nurture them wholly

I remember the day we left hospital after our first child was born. Before we could leave, a nurse was required to check that we had properly secured our tiny baby boy into the infant car seat. Bundled up for the chilly February ride home, our son looked like a football with a head attached to it. Being complete amateurs at parenting, we were glad when we received the nurse's approval on our bundling and buckling skills. After passing the test of securing him sufficiently, we were ready to go home.

She then handed us a single sheet of paper with instructions on diapering, feeding, and sleeping. She also asked if we had any questions. We both honestly had no idea what questions we should even ask, so mustering up as much confidence as we could fake, we lied and said we were good to go. If parenting could be summed up on a single piece of paper, we had better act like we got this and hope to convince her we should be trusted with this little life. It worked and she wished us the best. Still faking confidence, I casually folded the paper and stuck it in the diaper bag, and off we went on a most important life-long journey, completely clueless.

In the days, months, and years ahead my husband and I became far more comfortable in our abilities to care for little ones. This was mainly because we quickly realized we would need more guidance than that single piece of paper. We read many books, listened to tons of advice, asked endless questions of other parents, and prayed like crazy. Like most parents, as our family grew, so did our knowledge about child safety, nutrition, discipline, education, child development, and so on. And like most parents, we sought to create the best possible environment for our children to be healthy and safe. But that is far from all there is to parenting. From the first day we found out we were going to be parents, we knew we had the responsibility not only to nurture the physical health of the children the Lord would bring into our family, but also to nurture their spiritual and emotional health.

In light of this, we prayed even more. We prayed for ourselves and for our children regularly. We intentionally invested in teaching them about God in their day-to-day life. We sang songs about God and memorized his Word with them. We read and reread countless children's story Bibles and watched hours of VeggieTales. We also sought to faithfully live out in front of them what it means to follow Jesus, love God, and love others. Christian parents want nothing more than for their children to know and understand the gospel and to follow Jesus from a young age. So we invested in their spiritual health every day, knowing that there is more to life than just their physical well-being. Their flourishing is not only about tending to their physical bodies but about investing in their eternal souls.

Embracing the reality that children are embodied souls, we took seriously the stewardship to care for them both physically and spiritually. Intertwined in this was the understanding that we had a vital influence over and responsibility for their emotional health as well. This is why I encourage parents to nurture children wholly. Parents must attend to the whole life of the child. Just as we should attend to the physical care of a child, we should also attend to their spiritual and emotional care.

TIP 2

Understand their capacity

Attending to a child's emotional health looks different in the various ages and stages of a child's life. It is important to know your child's capacity at each stage of development. Understanding what is needed to care for a child's emotional health will vary from child to child to some degree, but some general guidance will help all parents.

The following is not a comprehensive instruction manual on child development. Much more can be and has been said on this subject. However, the next few pages give a brief snapshot on how to nurture your child's emotional health in relation to their growth and maturity.

Birth to age 3
The trek from infancy to toddlerhood
At these ages, emotions look like this:

- Communicating and expressing emotion manifests in general rather than specific ways. For example, crying can be a means to express pain, exhaustion, confusion, fear, and anger. Laughter can certainly be an expression of happiness, but it can also be a startle response, an expression of excitement, or a response to being entertained. An infant or toddler has few categories for expressing specific emotions, so parents have to do some detective work to uncover what the emotional expression really means.
- Children mirror the emotions of their caregivers. Your emotional responses as a parent therefore have a significant impact on teaching your little one about emotional health.
- Babies' and toddlers' emotions are also highly influenced by the people and environment to which they are immediately exposed.
- As children in this age group lack verbal communication, they will use their body to

express emotions. Startling, stiffening their body, facial expressions, and belly laughs or giggles can all be ways for them to do this.

Parents can do the following:

- Provide comfort and attention to the child's needs and emotional expressions.
- Begin identifying emotions by naming those you are seeing in the child. For example, "You are so happy!" "Are you sad?" and "Did that make you angry?" are all phrases that help very young children begin to identify their emotions.
- Correct or ignore emotional expressions cautiously. There can be times when correcting or disregarding emotional responses is an option in your parenting, but that approach is best when used infrequently. It can dismiss what the child is seeking to communicate and so can send the wrong message that emotions should be unheeded.

Parents are the sole source of the child's well-being. They provide everything children of this age need to thrive. Small children have little to no agency on what they need for their own health.

At this stage, children's reactions to fear are not the normal fight or flight response. They look to the parental response to teach them how to respond to threat. They look to parents for protection. It is important to attend to them physically with a loving and safe touch, as well as to responsively notice their expressions and reactions. Even though infants and toddlers don't have language to communicate their needs, questions, or emotions, that doesn't mean they don't communicate. Parents must be aware that their children are communicating needs, whether those are physical, emotional, or relational. The tricky part is that you may have to do some detective work to know what they are communicating.

I remember a time when my youngest son was about a year old and he would not sit still on my lap as we waited for an appointment. Though he was normally good about sitting with me, this time he was squirmy, fussy, and unwilling to comply. When I plopped him on my lap, he would immediately stiffen his body in refusal. He fidgeted and fussed through the appointment, asserting his will the whole time. When the appointment was over, he continued to be difficult all the way home. I was pretty frustrated by his behavior, so when we arrived home, I was more than ready for him to take his nap. As I checked his diaper before laying him down, I discovered what he was trying to communicate to me: a toddler-sized handful of Lego blocks were stuck to his tender baby butt cheeks!

Since he was still a young toddler, we did not allow him to play with the Legos with his older brother and sister because the bricks were small enough to create a choking risk. He must have found the forbidden blocks and tucked them away in the most secret place he could think of. Much to his chagrin, he ended up having to sit on them for the next hour. Without words, he was communicating to me as best he could his discomfort and displeasure. And without words, he was trying to keep his "stash" undetected. This certainly created an emotional conundrum for him. The expression on his face when I retrieved the blocks demonstrated that he felt guilty.

During the appointment, I assumed his fussing was willfulness and did not consider that there may have been another explanation for his actions. As I detached the blocks from his skin, it was clear the consequence for hiding the blocks was already sufficiently *felt*. Having sat on the unyielding blocks over the last hour, the many "Lego" logos that were now imprinted on his baby cheeks were punishment enough. While I affirmed to him in my words that those were "no-nos," I offered him care and comfort. Despite the self-inflicted consequence, I wanted him to know that I finally understood there was more to his cries and wiggles. This immediately resulted in him giving me the sweetest little bear hug, and I knew he felt understood.

In the midst of demanding days and sleepless nights, parents can be tempted to think that their baby or toddler is only acting out in disobedience or rebellion when expressing displeasure. While children in this age group certainly can be stubborn or defiant, it is important not to assume that this is always the case. They convey distress, discomfort, or confusion in some of the same ways they communicate other needs. If you only assume bad behavior, you run the risk of teaching them that their emotional cries of distress are only met with correction rather than comfort.

It is most important that a young child's emotional needs are met. When you notice your infant or toddler is emotionally distressed, prioritize comfort over correction. Attend to them with a gentle tone of voice and comforting physical contact. There will be plenty of times when correction is needed, but if correction is always your first and sometimes your only default response to your little one's cries, they will learn that expressing their needs (be it physical or emotional) is a negative thing. Bring comfort first, and you will find they are often more responsive to correction.

At this early age, your response to their distress affirms to them that you can be trusted to attend to them emotionally. In this, you are setting the stage for great conversations in the later years when they do have words. You are teaching them that their voice matters and that you will hear them in their distress.

Carrisa Quinn from the BibleProject explains the compassionate parenthood of God in this way: "God's compassion means that he is always turned toward us, like a good parent. . . . Because of his compassion, he always responds to the cries of his children. He is a God who cares deeply, emotionally, and consistently, like a loving parent."[4]

God gives us a picture of how he comforts us in our distress. He says to his people, "As a mother comforts her child, so will I comfort you" (Isaiah 66:13). No matter how young your child is, you are investing in their emotional health. With this verse in mind, you can offer this same comfort to your little ones, developing in them the foundations of emotional stability.

Ages 4 to 7
Emerging into early childhood

At these ages, emotions look like this:

- Children will have more ability to express and identify emotions.
- Play and imagination are key ways kids communicate their emotions.
- They will become aware of how their emotions impact and influence others.
- Children begin to empathize. This is a big change in their development and will impact how they respond to the emotional highs and lows of others.
- They begin to be more emotionally impacted by their playmates. They start to take things personally.

Understand their capacity

Parents can do the following:

- Provide encouraging and positive support of their child's feelings. Even if emotions are negative or expressed wrongly, a parent can supportively help the child toward other appropriate ways of expressing feelings, to see that they can have feelings without having to choose sinful responses. This will bring helpful clarification that emotions are not necessarily sinful but the way we choose to express them can be.

- Begin to ask simple questions about the child's thoughts and feelings: "What made you upset?" "Can you tell me how you feel?" "Can you put a name on the emotion you are feeling?" "How big is your emotion?" "What thoughts are in your mind as you are feeling _____?"

- Allow for personal expression of emotions at this stage. Some kids become physically needy in emotional distress. Others need to talk. Some need a little space to calm down.

- Help your child begin to strategize about how to better manage or respond to emotions. This helps them begin to move toward emotional regulation. Regulation is not suppressing emotion; rather, it is learning how to appropriately manage strong emotions. One way to help children regulate their emotions is to regulate with them. Engage in calming practices with them (breathing, relaxing, praying). This co-regulation teaches them how to soothe themselves when needed.

- Teach them that God will help them when they are struggling with strong feelings. Pray with them to help calm them down emotionally.

At this age, children have a developed language and agency. They begin to take on more responsibility in attending to their needs. Though still very dependent, they can recognize and appropriately respond to many of their physical needs by asking for help. Parents continue to be the primary provider of their child's overall well-being, but children become contributors to their own health as well. They develop empathy and often show it with little inhibition to those around them. They are old enough to offer care and support, and often offer it generously.

I remember seeing significant emotional development take place in my daughter when she was five years old. One of the ways I observed this was when my mother-in-law had intercepted a neighborhood cat in the midst of destroying a sparrow's nest. The damage was nearly a complete catastrophe except for one tiny baby hidden under some leaves. My mother-in-law set up a birdy ICU in a shoebox with the hope to provide care for the baby bird. As soon as my daughter saw this tiny orphan, she immediately expressed an intense investment to care for it. While I was endeared by her tender responses, in the back of my mind I felt a bit of dread because I knew that baby bird rescues don't often end well. I realized her powerful emotional response of care would likely end in an equally powerful response of grief. I am sad to say that this is exactly what happened.

As soon as she heard the baby bird had died, her eyes welled up with tears. Instead of clinging to me and crying, she went straight to her craft table and began to draw an elaborate picture of the little bird. In this moment, she was expressing her emotions in a way that she felt most comfortable doing. I could see that it would not be helpful for her to talk about it; she needed to express her emotions through art. And even as an adult, art is still a way she expresses herself.

Knowing how much emotional development is happening at this age, parents must wisely give guidance toward appropriate expressions of emotions in ways that fit their particular child.

Ages 8 to 11
The in-between years

At these ages, emotions look like this:

- ~~Expect emotional mood swings to begin~~. Around the age of nine, puberty begins and hormones are introduced in the brain at greater degrees. ~~Emotional reactions may seem too big or too small for the situation.~~ ~~Learning how to express and regulate emotions continues to be important for this age group.~~

- Children at this stage will look to their peers for emotional support and will begin to share emotions with their peers. Despite this, parental connection, influence, and affirmation is still vital for their emotional health.

- Independent thinking and agency are explored and expressed.

- Children can vocalize and share their emotional struggles more specifically.

Parents can do the following:

- Continue to help the child with emotion regulation. Avoid matching your child's emotional reaction. Instead, seek to temper situations and model self-control.
- Allow your child to share their emotions, and provide comfort and direction in these conversations. Listen to them when they open up, and avoid jumping quickly to instruction or correction. Even when you think you have listened long enough, listen longer.
- Be involved in their interactions with friends. Monitor and be very cautious with the use of any social media or online interactions in these years.
- Offer alternative actions and reactions when your child is emotionally upset. Children won't always have the ability to think of alternatives and will need help in discovering that they have choices even in the midst of their emotional distress.
- Encourage your child to talk to God through prayer or journaling when emotions are difficult to express. Show them how the Bible gives voice to emotions in the Psalms.

Have you ever been in a situation where someone was overreacting? My guess is you have, and it may have even been that you were the one overreacting. As a counselor, I worked with a couple I will call Jeff and Sue, who came to see me to get help walking with their nine-year-old daughter, who I will call Joy. She had always been a very expressive child, but entering fourth grade brought unexpected moods and emotions. These were unsettling to her parents, who were struggling to know how to best respond to her emotional outbursts.

One day, Jeff and Sue came to their counseling session and asked to talk about something unrelated to Joy. They wanted to talk about a recent argument between the two of them that had ended in Sue becoming offended and hurt. It started when Jeff decided to spend Saturday catching up on needed household chores despite Sue's plan to spend some quality time together as a family. A discussion ensued, which quickly escalated into a heated argument. Sue's disappointment turned to anger. When Jeff dismissed her emotions, calling them "reactionary," this only increased Sue's frustration. Jeff, exhausted by the conversation, vented his anger and frustration as well. This launched them into a full-blown conflict. It ended with Sue locking herself in her bedroom, ignoring both Jeff and Joy for the rest of the day.

Sitting in the counseling room with me, they both conceded to handling the situation poorly. Sue shared how she felt in that moment. She admitted that while she knew she was making too much of things, it felt like Jeff's response incited her to take things up a notch. Jeff also admitted that he was unwilling to back down, despite knowing this intransigence would make Sue more upset. I will spare you the details of that counseling session, but what I will share is how it ended because I think it may help parents know how to better respond to their children's emotional outbursts.

As we talked, I asked them what it would look like if they could "redo" that day. What resulted was very important, not just for their marriage but also for their parenting. They both explained that matching each other's emotional reactions was not helpful and only escalated the situation. When they began to discuss how they could have responded differently to one another, they shared that listening to each other would have de-escalated the situation even if they did not reach an agreement. While Sue knew she was overreacting, especially when she locked herself in the bedroom all day, she also acknowledged it was hard to change course. They both communicated how it was a challenge to not be led by their emotions when the other was equally amped up.

This led us to discuss their parenting. They recalled times when Joy had overreacted. They humbly shared how tempting they found it to respond in a way that matched their daughter's emotional distress with their own emotional frustration. If it was hard for them as adults to regulate and control their emotions, how much more for their nine-year-old child?

While this situation was an opportunity for them to grow as husband and wife, it was also a moment they grew as parents. They began to empathize with their daughter and made the connection of just how important it is for them to take the mature road of self-control when responding to Joy's emotions. In doing this, they can avoid sending Joy into a more escalated emotional response.

We can learn from this as well. Matching your child's emotional outburst is rarely helpful, especially when you know your child is overacting. Instead, it is important for parents to calm themselves and respond in a thoughtful and appropriate way. Not only does this model for the child what emotional control looks like, but it also can calm the child, creating space for a conversation about the emotions the child is feeling. Such co-regulation is an important skill to practice in this stage of development, as well as being a helpful marriage tip!

Isn't it nice to know that God doesn't freak out when we overreact? How many times do we come to the Lord in a fuss and fury about something, and he meets us with these words: "Be still and know that I am God" (Psalm 46:10). When I am emotionally amped up and wondering if things are going to be OK, he tells me nothing is too hard for him (Jeremiah 32:27).

Most people tend to think that parents can expect to be most engaged in fostering emotional health during the teenage years. After all, that is when we tend to expect the rush of emotions and impulsive actions to be most common. But don't underestimate the significance of this preteen stage in the emotional development of your child. Ron Dahl is director of the Institute for Human Development at the University of California,

Berkeley. He argues that this age is "the window to make a difference" when it comes to the emotional health of children.[5]

Ages 12 to 18
Advancing into adolescence
At these ages, emotions look like this:

- Children become more self-conscious and struggle emotionally with fitting in. They feel awkward and are overly concerned with their image.
- Often many questions about identity and sexuality arise in this stage, bringing emotional confusion.
- Teens often put pressure on themselves and can struggle when they don't live up to their own expectations.
- Mood swings are common, as are emotional outbursts.
- In the teen years, kids can become more emotionally guarded and can be hesitant to open up.
- Teens can have a judgmental attitude toward their parents' input and push back against rules for the sake of independence.

- They tend to be naturally entitled and are easily frustrated when their expectations are not met.
- Teens can be argumentative, but are also willing to stand on their own convictions. They can be impassioned to support a cause with which they empathetically connect.
- They long for acceptance and thrive on encouragement both from peers and parents.
- It is normal for kids in this stage to have increased stress and anxiety.

Parents can do the following:

- Recognize that much of what they are seeing is highly influenced by hormones. Your child's brain is seeing more hormones in the teen years than it ever has before. A little sympathy during these hormonal surges is helpful.
- Offer comfort during emotional lows. Affirm your support and willingness to be present.
- Be clear in your communication and in your expectations.
- Be consistent but gracious.
- Try not to take things personally.
- When you have to bring correction or

consequences, affirm your love for them sincerely. Help them to think through long-term consequences rather than immediate satisfaction.

- Be sensitive to their struggle with insecurity. Point them to the unshakable identity that is theirs in Christ.
- Provide positive feedback and encourage them regularly.
- Model loving responses and interactions. Live out concrete actions of faith in front of them.

Have you ever arranged to rent a particular car, but been given an upgrade when you arrived to pick it up? This has happened to me recently. I was upgraded to a car that had several new driver-assistance features. These safety features allow the car to respond for you while you drive. For example, when you start to move toward the edge of a lane, the car detects that you are drifting and gently but persistently inhibits you from moving out of your lane. The vehicle upgrade I received not only had this feature, but was also able to detect how close I was to the car in front of me. It would speed up or slow down to maintain the safest distance from other drivers. This car was so capable of deterring me from getting too close to another driver that when the car in front of me unexpectedly came to a complete stop, so did my car—without my ever touching the brake! This automatic counteraction has the potential to prevent many accidents and injuries. What does all this have to do with teens and emotional well-being? Let me explain.

Brain development continues for most of our lives, but significant growth and development culminates when frontal lobes become mature. The prefrontal cortex, the area of the brain responsible for executive brain function, is only just beginning to develop in adolescence and doesn't reach full development until around age twenty-five.[6] This part of our brain is responsible for inhibition. Like the car I rented, the prefrontal cortex wisely assesses and evaluates situations, and provides us with the most reasonable responses to keep us safe and alive. While the prefrontal cortex is developmentally immature in the teen years, the nucleus accumbens is fully developed in the teenage brain. This region of the forebrain is associated with pleasure seeking. This means that the part of the brain that sends dopamine rewards to reinforce pleasurable experiences is at full operation, while the logical and rational part of the brain that sends messages of needed inhibition is only just beginning to become more operational. The combined effect of these two realities of brain development is explained by Bill Bryson in his book *The Body: A Guide for Occupants*. He says that, in the teen years, "the body produces more dopamine, the neurotransmitter that conveys pleasure, than it ever will again. That is why the sensations you feel as a teenager are more intense than at any other time of life. But it also means that seeking pleasure is an occupational hazard for teenagers."[7]

In other words, teens will be deeply moved by things and yet have poor judgment on how to respond to those feelings. They can be impassioned and impulsive, making decisions based on their feelings rather than on logic and reasoning. It is good for parents to keep this in mind when raising teens. Teenage emotions are always changing, and their brains are trying to keep up. They don't have the rationale needed to slow down and consider. Their driver-assistance package is not yet fully installed. This is where your guidance is vital. Teens need gracious shepherding from those who understand their brain is still developing. Parents should seek to provide direction with a grace-filled understanding of this phenomenon.

Author Frances Jensen offers this helpful advice: "Your children are changing, and also trying to figure themselves out; their brains and bodies are undergoing extensive reorganization; and their apparent recklessness, rudeness, and cluelessness is not totally their fault! Almost all of this is neurologically, psychologically, and physiologically explainable. As a parent or educator, you need to remind yourself of this daily, often hourly!"[8] But this does not mean they get a free pass on bad behavior. She goes on to explain that it is appropriate for teens to hear that "your brain is sometimes an explanation; it's never an excuse."[9]

With a better understanding of the neurological development of this age group, parents can provide appropriate responses to a teen's emotional reactions. Offering compassionate guidance can set the stage for continued meaningful conversations.

No matter your child's age or stage, attending to their emotional needs will include being intentionally present with them. It means spending quality time with them. It requires engaging them at their level while understanding their limits.

Now that you have an overview of what emotional development can look like in children at various ages and stages, the rest of this book will be focused on how to foster emotional health in your child. The following tips will help you to raise emotionally healthy kids. They are not a checklist of things to do once. Rather, they are a lifestyle for you to embrace through the years of parenting.

TIP 3

Regard their feelings

One way to raise emotionally healthy kids is to give appropriate regard to your child's feelings. Underreacting or overreacting to your child's emotions creates an environment that is not conducive to healthy interaction. Wise, gentle responses express respectful regard for how your child feels. Even if their emotional responses need correction, a grace-filled response opens the door for fruitful guidance toward healthier expressions.

Regarding their feelings can be tricky when each day can be a roller-coaster of emotions for a child. This reality can tempt parents to disregard or ignore their child's emotional responses. You may feel your child is "too sensitive" or "overreacts,"

Or you may assume that if your child doesn't show that they are bothered, they are just fine. Or you may feel that responding to your child's poor emotional reactions will only encourage such reactions. Wisdom is certainly needed. But, in general, your parenting should communicate that you want to understand the feelings your child is experiencing. Allow this to be what permeates your parenting. By not making the effort to understand your child's feelings, you can end up simply telling your child how they should feel while disregarding their actual feelings. This can inadvertently teach the child to suppress their true feelings and simply accept what others say they should feel.

Regarding your child's emotions is also significant because it can open opportunities to address their heart. Emotional expressions reveal what's going on in the heart. No matter how old the child is, their heart will overflow in their emotional reactions. Emotions are therefore often the entry gates to deeper, meaningful conversations. You can begin to regard your child's emotions by responding considerately to them and asking engaging questions.

If you view your reactions to your child's feelings as teaching moments and provide understanding guidance, they will learn how to respond better to you and others. You will be modeling for them what it means to be empathetic. Empathy does not mean that you agree with everything a person feels. It simply recognizes the significance of the feelings they are experiencing and seeks to be present with them. ~~By regarding your children's feelings, you communicate that what they are going through matters to you as their parent.~~ You are communicating that you are interested in what they are facing, willing to hear their experience, and invested in being with them through it.

In this way, you model Jesus, who met people in their pain and discomfort. He cared for people even when their suffering was caused by poor choices they made. He was moved with compassion when people's suffering came from external situations. He wept when people grieved; he rejoiced with people at celebrations. He was tender with little children, who certainly had childish emotional reactions. He did not always correct people. In fact, especially with the most vulnerable, Jesus sought to understand and care for them. In doing this, he won the people's hearts. As a result, these wounded and hurting people wanted to be with him, to share life with him, and to follow him. As a parent, let Jesus be your example of respectfully regarding people's feelings.

It is easy to trivialize a child's emotional response, especially when what they are upset about is a trifle. In these situations, ask engaging questions. Doing this not only shows regard for their feelings, but also communicates to your child that you are committed to knowing them as a person, even when they don't always make sense. Sometimes kids know they are overreacting, but don't always know how to correct their course. Your gracious and engaging questions provide opportunities for them to express themselves differently. ~~By asking questions to help you understand your child better, you can also help your child understand themselves better.~~

Socrates knew this very well. He used questions to help his students move toward an understanding of themselves and their world. Engaging questions can lead a child toward exploring what is behind the deep emotions they are feeling. "Sometimes asking a few questions can open the door for more receptive hearts and minds," says Randy Newman, author of *Bringing the Gospel Home*.[10] Again, Jesus is your example in asking engaging questions. It is noteworthy to see just how many times in the Bible we see Jesus asking questions yet answering few. His questions were often meant to simply engage the person. Let that be your goal as you seek to ask your child about their emotions. Ask more; answer less.

For some parents, this will come naturally, but many find it challenging to know how to ask questions that draw your child out. Here are a handful of questions that can help you begin to engage with your child. You can use them as conversation starters the next time you are seeking to attend to your child in their emotional distress.

Questions to ask younger children

- Start by asking them to name their feelings. Give them plenty of space before suggesting emotions they may be feeling because emotions are often mixed or confusing. When they name an emotion, simply acknowledge it, then ask, "What else are you feeling?" or "Is there anything else you feel?" This is important because, for example, sometimes sadness can feel like anger and excitement can feel like nervousness. If the emotion they name does not match what you see, gently offer a suggestion. You can also use a feelings wheel to help your child name their emotions.

- Ask them to measure their feelings. This can be done by drawing a line on a piece of paper, with one point marked "0," which equals zero distress, and the other point marked "10," which indicates maximum distress. Alternatively, use your hand to indicate a distance. First, ask your child to measure or rate how upset they are. Then ask, "What would move your emotions closer or above 10?" and "What would move your emotions closer to zero?"

- Ask your child to identify where they feel their emotions in their body. This can be done by asking, "How does your body know that you are _____ [name the emotion they shared]?" Or you could inquire, "You are very upset right now. Where does your body feel it the most?" Talk about how it feels and what might help it to feel better. Consider taking a few deep breaths with them to calm their body. Encourage your child to pretend that they are blowing bubbles from a bubble wand to facilitate deep breathing.

- If their emotions are obvious, or you both have named what they are feeling, empathize with them: "I can see you are excited about your friend coming over. It is so fun to be with friends!" Or, "You were hurt by what your classmate said at school today. It would hurt me too if someone said that to me."

Questions to ask older children and teens

- If you have a teen who doesn't easily open up, try saying, "I am sorry you are struggling. I love you and am here for you. You don't have to give me the details, but would you mind simply sharing with me what emotion you feel most right now?" You can then ask if they want to share more. Even if they do not, make sure to thank them for what they did share.
- "Is there anything you want to talk about that might be hard to say?"
- "You look happy! I would love to hear what has made you feel good."
- "You seem sad. I am interested to know what is making you seem down."
- "If you could magically change one thing right now to make your situation a little better, what would it be?" After they name it, ask them, without judgment, to consider the pros and cons of that change. How would the change impact them and others in their life?

For children of all ages

When kids are in the midst of emotional distress, offer comfort or coping options before seeking to discuss their emotions. Ask the child what they think might help calm them down. Then offer a couple of options, including some either/or ones:

- "Can I sit with you?"
- "Can I sit with you or would you rather have some space?"
- "Would you like me to pray for you right now?"
- "How about we pray together? Or, if you want, I can just pray for you?"
- "Do you want me to give you a hug?"
- "Can I read a passage of Scripture that might comfort you?"
- "How about we take a few deep breaths together?"

Do not underestimate either the power of caring for their body. Consider whether they are overheated or whether it would help for them to change into more comfortable clothes. You can also ask whether they would like to take a little rest or whether you can make them something to eat.

When you regard your child's emotions, it communicates that their emotions matter. It also helps them to know emotions need to be explored and examined. ~~Your engaging questions tell them that you are interested and invested in what they are experiencing. You are communicating that their struggle does not mean they are a problem to be solved but a person to be understoo~~d. This lays the foundation for good emotional health.

Before attempting to rush into conversations, take a moment by yourself to pray and then be sure to keep praying in your spirit during the conversations with your child. Trust God to work in these conversations and seek to emulate Jesus. In all of this, you are communicating to your child that you are a trusted person who will help them in their troubles.

TIP 4

Cultivate lasting hope

The world in which children are growing up is full of uncertainties and challenges. Kids are bombarded with negative messages and fear-inducing news from the internet and social media. Stories of hate, war, crime, heartache, and trauma are available at their fingertips from a phone, laptop, or tablet. This reality is having an impact on their emotional well-being. Seeing these early trends, the American Psychological Association stated in an article published in 2018 that "adolescents who spent more time on new media (including social media and electronic devices such as smartphones) were more likely to report mental health issues, and adolescents who spent more time on non-screen activities (in-person social interaction, sports/exercise, homework, print media, and attending religious services) were less likely."[11]

Long before the internet and smartphones, the television was the only screen that exposed kids to the larger world and all its troubles. I was one of those kids. For me, the majority of what I watched consisted of sitcoms or Saturday morning cartoons. The only hints of the world came to me in glimpses of news which felt mostly like boring grown-up TV. However, when I was a teen, a new show aired called *Cops*, and it hooked me. In many ways, it was the first reality TV show, and I watched it regularly. I can still sing the theme song: "Bad boys, bad boys, whatcha gonna do? Whatcha gonna do when they come for you?" The show's popularity launched the production of similar shows, making this genre even more available to watch.

The entire content of these shows was live footage of police officers as they patrolled or responded to 911 emergency calls. Armed with body cameras, these officers gave the watching world an up-close look at the crime happening in our neighborhoods. For me, the shows were captivating and crippling. They were captivating because of the intensity of what unfolded. I could feel the adrenaline of the officers as they flipped on their lights and sirens or ran after someone in a foot chase. Yet it was also crippling because it removed my blinders of innocence about the safety of the world in which I was living. Instead of being carefree when I was out and about, I grew much more suspicious and on guard. Being home alone at night became a recipe for endless anxiety. After a night of watching those shows, nightmares followed.

I ended up making the decision to completely stop watching police shows. I realized I was absorbing stories and images that were only making me anxious. As a teen, it was one of the wisest decisions I ever made. It took a little while, but slowly the stories of "life on the beat" became less present in my mind and my anxiety eventually decreased.

Today, the internet and social media provide numerous provocations of anxiety for kids. But kids and teens of the twenty-first century are dealing with more than just anxiety. Depression, insecurity, identity issues, stress, self-hate, self-harm, phobias, traumatization, and many other struggles have become common mental health issues for them. The ubiquitous nature of screens in a child's life means potential endless exposure to messages that contribute to poor mental health, most specifically through social media.

While research reveals an increase in adolescents suffering from a diagnosable mental health disorder, it also indicates that "the increase has coincided with the widespread adoption of social media."[12] But researchers are not the only ones making the link. Kids themselves affirm this connection. Almost 25% of adolescents believe that social media has a mostly negative effect,[13] and that number is starting to increase. However, it is not increasing nearly as quickly as the number of kids who say they use social media every day, which increased by 40% in four years according to the research.[14] Overall, kids between the ages of eight and twelve years old spend close to five hours a day on screen media, and teens spend over seven hours on screen media (not including school-related screen use).[15] The excessive amount of time connected to a screen has raised concern that addiction is another mental health struggle that children are facing.

All of this can leave parents feeling uncertain about what to do. Social media is often the main avenue of connection for their kids, and the internet is usually a necessary part of a child's everyday life. This dilemma is what motivated me to write *Raising Kids in a Screen-Saturated World*.[16] For more specific help in navigating screen balance, I commend that book to you. However, for our purposes here, we are going to focus less on how families can wisely use screens. Instead, our main focus will be how to cultivate hope for kids living in the constant barrage of negative messages that come mainly in digital form.

Even if your child has limited screen use, they will still encounter hope-altering realities in life. Life is a mix of the good and the difficult, and children are not immune to troubles or suffering. The global pandemic that began in 2020 is a good example of this. Every school-aged child experienced for well over a year what it is like to live in a constant state of uncertainty and threat.

But kids don't have to be going through a pandemic to feel hopeless. There are many situations in the world today that can cause kids to feel hopeless. Pressures from peers, problems in the family, tension to perform or achieve, fears about their life, and stress about the future can trouble young minds. They don't need to look far to see crime, protests, divisions, and hate. It can feel like the world is an unsafe place. Children also now have a much greater awareness of mental health issues and all of the related symptoms. All of this contributes to emotional struggles.

In turn, parents are left wondering what they can do to cultivate hope and bolster their child's emotional health. They ask themselves whether there is a way to shelter their child from the difficulties they may face in this life.

You may not always be able to wrap your child in your arms and tell them everything will be alright. However, the simple acronym ARMS can help you cultivate needed hope in their young hearts. Use it as you seek to care for their emotional health.

A   *Assure* **them of your consistent love**. As your child faces emotional ups and downs, affirm to them your consistent love. This is important even if you think your child knows you love them. Tell them again. Consider what great lengths the Lord has undertaken to affirm his love for us. He sent his Son and then wrote down in the Bible the story of his love for us to read again and again. If God assures and reassures us of his love, we can follow his example by doing the same for our struggling children.

R   *Remind* **them of God's faithfulness.** We all benefit from being reminded of God's faithfulness, but the reminders are more needed when we are struggling. Point your child to the care, rescue, provision, and comfort that God has provided in the past, as well as to his promises to do so in the future. Share your own stories of God's faithfulness to you in your life as a child. Take an additional step of vulnerability by sharing present stories of his faithfulness. Never underestimate how sharing God's love for you in your own dark moments can be used by God. It can open avenues of discussion and healing for you both. Use Scripture to remind them of God's faithfulness.

M   *Meditate* **on capital "T" truths with them.** It might be true that things are difficult for your child right now, but what else is true? It is perfectly fine to acknowledge the hard truths that are happening. It is right to recognize that your child's present situation is painful or difficult. However, help them recognize that these truths are lowercase "t" truths. While true, they are not *all* that is true. There are greater eternal truths. These capital "T" truths are timeless and unaffected by troubles. It is easy for their minds to fixate on the painful negative "truths" and leave little space for hopeful eternal "Truths." Use Scripture to meditate on these eternal truths together. To give you a little guidance, some helpful verses are Psalm 34:18, Isaiah 43:1–5, Lamentations 3:21–23 and Philippians 4:6–7.

S   *Seek* **to be a blessing.** Serving and blessing others can bring a much-needed change of scenery when life is discouraging. Look for opportunities to bring light and joy to others by serving together as a family. This shift of focus allows kids to be a part of helping others and, in small ways, brings hopeful change to their world. You can serve in your church or your community, but you can also serve the people in your life already. Consider how you might engage your child in encouraging their family members and friends (near and far), or in blessing the people who live in your neighborhood. Remind them that serving others is one of the ways God blesses us and has called us to be a blessing.

Use this acronym to guide you as you seek to care for your child and encourage them toward the hope that is theirs in Christ. The best hope you can hold out for your child is the hope that is anchored on the unchanging truth of God's Word in the gospel. Whether or not your child has confessed faith in Christ, they need to hear of the supreme hope found in Christ. Remind them of the love God demonstrated in sending Jesus and of the power that the gospel holds to make all things new again.

The gospel is is the answer to the question Samwise Gamgee asks in J. R. R. Tolkein's *The Hobbit*: "Is everything sad going to come untrue?" Yes, Samwise, yes it will! God has a perfect plan to redeem the world and give us a future where pain, sorrow, sin, and brokenness are no more. And he accomplished this through the sending of Jesus to live and die for us. In Christ, we have hope that everything sad will come untrue. In that renewed creation, there will be no police shows highlighting the brokenness around us because all things will be made new and right; it will be a world of perfect peace (Revelation 21:4–5).

While you seek to cultivate hope in your child, do the same for yourself. Nothing can be more discouraging than watching your child struggle or suffer. Parents need hope as well. So use this same acronym to cultivate hope in your own life. Remind yourself of the unchanging promises of God and of the confidence of better days that the gospel brings. Build that hope in your own life.

TIP 5

Attend to yourself

"Is it contagious?" This short question carried great significance for our family one summer. We had taken a vacation with our extended family and were enjoying the continual company of multiple generations, all under one roof. The memories made were filled with laughter and fun. But during the vacation, one of our children became sick—sick enough to warrant us returning home early. After a few doctor visits, we found out what was wrong. The diagnosis was pertussis, or whooping cough, a sickness I had heard of but knew very little about. Knowing we had just been in very close quarters with so many other family members, I asked those three words: "Is it contagious?" I knew I needed to determine if any of our extended family were now at risk.

The answer to the brief question put the wheels in motion for many calls to our family. We needed to inform them that they had indeed been exposed to a contagious and potentially serious illness. Our entire family was impacted by our child's sickness. This is the reality about contagious diseases. Until a diagnosis has been made, often we don't even know that we are potentially compromising someone's physical health.

To some degree, the same can be said of our emotional health. Mental illness is not contagious, but our emotional health has an impact on those around us. Emotionally healthy children are often the product of emotionally healthy parents. This is not to say that if your child is struggling emotionally, it is a direct reflection of your health. Nor is it to say that taking care of yourself is a guarantee that your children will not struggle emotionally. Parents should not feel guilt or shame when a child struggles. On the other hand, though, do understand that your emotional health matters to your child's well-being.

Children can perceive the emotional health of their parents. Part of this may come from the natural influence environment has on children, and part may be due to mirror neurons. The latter are why we flinch when we see others hurt themselves, why we laugh at a baby's giggle, and why we get teary when we see loved ones cry. Mirror neurons have been described as "embodied stimulation."[17] Emotional, and sometimes physical, reactions occur in our bodies when "seeing the emotions of others also recruits regions (of the brain) involved in experiencing similar emotions."[18] To varying degrees, we mirror the emotional health of those around us.

Attending to your emotional health as a parent is therefore very important. It can be helpful to take an inventory on how you are doing emotionally and then seek to make any necessary changes. Take a minute to read over the self-assessment below. If most of the statements describe you, then you are likely an emotionally healthy person. If reading the statements reveals areas where you struggle, or causes discouragement or distress, it may be an indication that greater investment in your emotional health is needed. Consider talking over the list with a trusted friend, a pastor, or a counselor for help in the areas you feel need attention. Taking a step toward better emotional health is a gift you give to your children.

Emotional wellness self-assessment

An emotionally healthy person:

1. **Views their limits appropriately.** You understand the value of asking for help and do so regularly. Rather than fighting your limits, you accept them. Realizing that God created us as dependent creatures, you allow others to support and assist you.
2. **Responds with fitting motivation.** You make decisions out of thoughtful, deliberate, willing, and compassionate wisdom, rather than out of a sense of obligation, resentfulness, or guilt.
3. **Takes care of their body**. You prioritize your physical needs for rest, exercise, and healthy nourishment, and attend to those needs through regular self-care. For specific direction on this, I have written *The Whole Life*, a book focused on biblical self-care.[19]
4. **Is in touch with their emotions.** Rather than suppressing emotions, you notice what you are experiencing and allow yourself to

feel and process. You can recognize when your emotions are helping or hurting the situation and make proper adjustments.

5. **Has healthy relationships.** You invest in life-giving relationships and place fitting boundaries around relationships that are emotionally destructive.

6. **Is flexible.** You are able to adjust when change occurs, and appropriately accept and adapt when things do not go as planned.

7. **Leans into personal growth.** You recognize that you are a work in progress and that God is not finished with you yet. This leads you to pursue growth in all areas of your life (including your spiritual, relational, physical, and emotional growth and development).

8. **Finds their worth in Christ.** You do not rely on the approval of others but rest in who you are in Christ. The opinions of others are filtered through the truth of Scripture and weighed with discernment.

9. **Avoids ruminating on failures.** You know the importance of forgiveness and fight the temptation to ruminate on what others have done. You also fight a defeatist mentality about your own mistakes by trusting that

God uses all things for his glory and for your good.

10. **Prioritizes regular time with the Lord.** You know that your emotional health is directly related to your spiritual health and so prioritize regular times in prayer and the Word.

Even emotionally healthy parents need help and support. Parenting is not easy. It can take a toll on you. But you are not alone. Lean into the church or your friends and family to find support, and attend to your own needs. This will, in turn, help you to be best prepared to attend to your children's needs.

The most beneficial help doesn't come from a parenting book. God has given you his Spirit and his Word. The Word of God is an abundant source of help, hope, and encouragement. It is tempting to parent while leaning on your own understanding, but Proverbs 3:5–6 gives better direction: "Trust in the LORD with all your heart and lean not on your own understanding; in all your ways submit to him, and he will make your paths straight." God will faithfully guide you by his Spirit as you parent. His ever-present help is available to you. By attending to your emotional health and relying on God's help, you are more likely to parent from a place of emotional health.

TIP 6

Know when to get help

Early one Monday morning, I got a text from the headmaster of a local high school: "I am about to call you, please answer." In the past, I had supported that school in their need for counseling, and had since become friends with the headmaster. His simple message gave me great concern. As my phone rang, I knew that my plans for the day were about to change, so I quickly prayed before answering.

"Eliza," he said in a serious and concerned tone, "a student attempted suicide this morning at the school. Can you come?" I hung up the phone and drove to the school where I heard the rest of the story.

The student, arriving at school very early that morning, had attempted to hang themself in a stairwell. Thankfully, and by God's grace, the rope broke and the student sustained only minor injuries. A few other students, who had come to school early for practice, heard the fall and went to investigate. Encountering their classmate on the ground and realizing what had happened, they called for help. The headmaster did an excellent job of triaging the situation, but certainly one of the hardest things to do was to call the parents of the suicidal student. Despite their relief that the suicide attempt was unsuccessful, no parent wants to hear that their child just attempted to end their life.

You may have picked up this book for general direction or precautionary help in your effort to raise emotionally healthy kids. Maybe you were looking for wisdom on what you can do to continue to support your child through the ups and downs of life. I hope it has been helpful. But for others, this book grabbed your attention because you have a child who is struggling emotionally. Maybe you have received a call like the parents from the story above. Or perhaps you worry that one day you will. In this final chapter, we will look at how to know when your child's emotional struggles have turned into a mental health crisis and when to get help.

The Association for Child Mental Health describes a mental health crisis as, "any time that your child is no longer safe to himself or others or when there is a need for immediate action or intervention. It is usually a time when all of your energies are being demanded in order to care for your child."[20] This definition is helpful, but many parents are still unsure how to tell if their child is struggling to the point of needing help. Therefore, some common signs to be aware of are listed below. Note that some of these signs can be related to other physical health issues. However, if there is no medical explanation and your child is exhibiting multiple signs, it is wise to consider getting them additional care.

How do I know if my child is struggling?
Physical signs:

- Unexplainable headaches or stomachaches.
- Sleep changes, such as excessive sleep, insomnia, or nightmares.
- Self-injury, such as cutting, burning, or hitting themselves.

- Attempts or desires to end their life.
- Change in appetite, whether an unexplained increase or decrease.
- Increased heartrate or a feeling like their heart is pounding.
- Feeling of a tight chest or difficulty breathing.
- Bedwetting (in younger children).

Emotional signs:

- Depressed mood.
- Mood swings.
- Loss of interest in things they normally enjoyed.
- Overreaction to minor disappointments or stresses.
- Difficulty in regulating or managing their emotions.
- Decline in their school performance or ability to focus.
- Clinginess (in younger children).
- Temper tantrums, hyperactivity, increased disobedience, or aggression (in younger children).

Relational signs:

- Difficulty adjusting to changes in life or in family life.
- Unusual withdrawal from close friends or family.
- Problems at school or with classmates.
- Social isolation.
- Risky behaviors.
- Sudden change in moral convictions.
- Experimentation with drugs or alcohol.
- Aggression with friends or family members (especially in younger children but in any age).

These key signs may be a helpful guide to determine if your child's mental health has reached a point where more serious action is needed. If you feel your child's emotional struggles have reached a crisis, here are some things you can do to help.

Stay calm

As we mentioned in the previous chapter, your emotions impact your child. Staying calm may be one of the most effective things you can do to help them. Dr Mark Mayfield, a Christian and mental health expert, explains, "If you can remain calm, it will provide space for your emotionally tumultuous child to experience calm. On the other hand, if you escalate your emotional status in front of your child, that excitability has the potential to escalate the situation."[21]

Pray

One of the best ways you can stay calm is by taking the time to pray. Ask the Lord to help you respond in a way that diffuses and disarms your child. With appropriate respect to privacy, ask others to pray for you and your child as well. The Lord hears our prayers and attends to our cry for help (Psalm 34:17).

Breathe

Another way to calm yourself and your child is to breathe. If you find yourself in an acute situation related to your child's mental health, give yourself a minute to take some slow deep breaths. This increases the supply of oxygen to the brain, which activates the parasympathetic nervous system in the brain, which then sends messages to the body to calm down and relax. Breathe on your own or with your child.

Consult

Get input from others. If possible, talk to someone else before you talk with your child—ideally, someone with experience in caring for mental health. When you do this, you give yourself space to process the situation. It also allows the input of others, who are less emotionally distressed by the situation, to guide you. All this helps you to respond out of a place of calm reason rather than rattled chaos.

Ensure safety
Assess

If you feel your child is in immediate danger to themselves or to others, and the risk is not something you feel you can take care of, prioritize safety and get appropriate help. Express to your child the concerns you are seeing and why you feel help is needed. If you are unsure if your child is suicidal, don't be afraid to ask. This will not put the idea into their head, nor will it make them at greater risk. In fact, the opposite is true: it lowers the risk because the seriousness of the situation is out in the open and the appropriate help and intervention can be provided. When people who are contemplating suicide are asked if that is the case, they are usually honest. Ask directly yet compassionately. For example, you can say, "You seem very impacted by your situation. Has it ever been so bad that you thought about dying or ending your life?" Or, "Do you ever think about more permanent ways of getting out of the situation, like ending your life?" You also want to assess the degree of imminence by determining if a plan has been made or if there is access to means. These are terribly hard questions to ask your child, but doing so means the danger is no longer hidden and you are now able to get the help that is needed.

Call

In situations where your child has expressed a threat to their own life or you have discovered they have made efforts to end their life, it is crucial to get urgent help. Call the emergency services (911 in America and 999 in the UK) or a crisis intervention hotline, or take your child to the hospital.

It can be helpful to know what will happen when you reach out for emergency help. In most cases, someone will be sent to you. It is important to let them know that you are calling about a child or teen as sometimes a person specially trained to work with children can be sentcome. Dr Mayfield again provides helpful input on this, suggesting that you also request no lights or sirens be used, if possible, when the emergency services are responding. When help arrives, they will determine the next steps to provide the best care and ensure safety.

If crisis care workers determine your child is not safe or needs additional care, they will take them to hospital. If the medical team at the hospital determines your child is not safe, they will likely require a hospital stay of two–three days to continue to assess your child. This ensures the situation is stabilized and avenues of continued care are secured. During this time, your child will receive both medical and psychiatric care and evaluation. In most cases, a counseling appointment must be scheduled with a professional counselor before the child is released from care. Parents can determine which counselor they want their child to see. A well-equipped, faith-based, biblical counselor, who is trained to work with kids and teens, is a good option where available.

Respond wisely
De-escalate

If you assess that your child is safe and external care is not necessary, try to respond in a way that de-escalates the situation. There are several ways to decrease the emotional intensity of a situation when a child is deeply struggling.

Firstly, avoid challenging their thoughts, feelings, or words. This is especially important when what they say is illogical, irrational, or even offensive. In an emotional crisis, kids (and adults for that matter) will sometimes say things that seem like personal attacks on you. These aggressive remarks can provoke you to respond defensively. You may be tempted to get sidetracked by the disrespectful ranting and feel like correction is most needed in that moment. However, while respecting you is important, your child's emotional stability should take precedence over discipline or consequences in that moment.

Secondly, avoid reacting to their behavior and take a moment to consider how you want to respond. Don't raise your voice or talk at an increased speed. Don't flex your authority. Don't argue or pressurize them. Don't threaten or give a verbal attack in return. Instead, talk to them in a gentle tone of voice. Whatever you say, speak softly and empathetically. Use positive words and affirm your love for them. Even while you disapprove of their actions, put that emotion on hold and respond in love. With grace and gentleness, let them know you want to help them. Be willing to listen patiently to what they are experiencing. Let them know too that they are not alone and that you will be with them. Confirm the Lord's love and presence with them. Reassure them that struggling emotionally does not make them a terrible kid or crazy person. Without being dismissive, help them to know that other kids have felt the same way. Seek to offer comfort and ask them what might help. (Refer back to the lists in TIP 2 for questions you can ask.)

Be patient

Be patient and constant in prayer as you seek help. Patience can sometimes be the hardest thing to embrace when your child is struggling emotionally. Parents want results today. They want change fast. It is important to accept that God may have more work to do and that learning to wait for his timing is part of that work.

Likewise, be patient with your child's counseling. There are many professionally trained counselors who are believers. They will counsel your child in a way that aligns with your faith while addressing the unique challenges your child is facing. But keep in mind that counseling takes time. Avoid putting timelines or expectations on the care your child is receiving. This will look different in each situation and will require prayerful wisdom and patience in you. God is not only working in your child's life, but is working in your own heart as well. Your posture of patient and humble teachability is a significant part of effective parenting.

Finally, I want to stress the importance of not going through a mental health crisis alone. Getting help can be done in a way that honors your child's privacy while informing people who are well-suited to offer care and support for you and your child.

Conclusion

I hope that in reading this book, you feel more equipped to nurture and care for your child's emotional health. I encourage you to prayerfully consider how what you have learned might help in your parenting. These final few paragraphs acknowledge that raising emotionally healthy kids is no simple task. Sometimes, even our most intentional efforts do not prevent our children from facing significant struggles. Since these closing words are so important to hold on to as you continue parenting your child through emotional ups and downs, read them slowly.

First, please remember that this small book is but one small resource. Much like that single piece of paper my husband and I received the day we were sent home from the hospital with our first child, there is no way to contain all the help parents need in just these few short chapters. Continue to seek support and direction from parents who have gone before you. Seek wisdom from pastors who shepherd your souls and the souls of your children. Prayerfully ask the Lord for wisdom. Don't underestimate the value of time with trained counselors to help both you and your children. I love the words of the late David Powlison who said simply, "Here is the sweet paradox in how God works. He blesses those who admit they need help."[22] Seeking help can be the very avenue that the Lord uses to care for you and your child.

Second, I want to acknowledge that extenuating circumstances sometimes cause children to be at a disadvantage regarding their emotional health. If your child has been exposed to significant trauma, been a victim of sexual abuse, or has a family history of mental illness, they may struggle more than other children. Also, physical illness or medications can sometimes cause kids to be at greater risk of mental health struggles. If your child has a chronic illness, a learning difference, or a health issue that significantly affects their life, it is not uncommon for their mental health to be impacted. In addition, children who have been adopted out of less-than-ideal situations may face more struggles emotionally. This can be correlated to various circumstances such as attachment-related issues, exposure to drugs in utero, or neglect. That is not to say that if any of these are in your child's history, they are sure to struggle emotionally. God is a redeeming and healing God. It is not too much for him to take your child's painful past and turn it into a story of blessing and beauty, free from deep emotional struggles. But that is not always how God chooses to work and sometimes significant emotional struggles are unavoidable.

Finally, I feel it is very important to pause and emphasize this next point. If your child is struggling emotionally, it does not make you a bad parent. Read that sentence again. One more time. The fact that you are reading this book demonstrates quite the opposite. As you continue to learn and seek out wisdom on how to love and care for your struggling child, resist any temptation to believe that it is all your fault. Fight off self-condemning shame. Every prayer you pray and every effort you make to wisely love and care for your child's emotional health is evidence that you are a good parent. The outcome of all parenting must be entrusted to God.

With those things in mind, I want to close this book the same way I opened it: with a prayer for you. Know that I have prayed it for each person who will ever hold this book in their hands. Receive it, knowing that God is able to do far more abundantly than we can ever ask or imagine in our lives and in the lives of our children. Let us trust him together.

Dear Father,
You are our loving and perfect parent. You tenderly care for us when we are struggling, and you guide us with your wisdom when we don't know what to do. Help the ones holding this book to trust you with the children they are raising. As they read this prayer, bring encouragement to their heart through your promise that you finish the good work you start. Grant them renewed faith in the situations that seem impossible, knowing that nothing is too difficult for you. Let their hearts be confident that you are with them in whatever challenges they face and that you will help them. I pray their children will be drawn to Jesus and may they have comfort, peace, and joy in knowing him.
It is in Jesus' name I pray for them, amen.

References

Why read this book?

1. Steinberg, Laurence, "Anxiety and Depression in Adolescence" (Child Mind Institute, March 12, 2021): childmind.org/report/2017-childrens-mental-health-report/anxiety-depression-adolescence/

2. Devitt, Michael, "Study: One in Six U.S. Children Has a Mental Illness" (American Academy of Family Physicians, March 18, 2019): www.aafp.org/news/health-of-the-public/20190318childmentalillness.html

3. Geiger, A. W., and Leslie Davis, "A Growing Number of American Teenagers—Particularly Girls—Are Facing Depression" (Pew Research Center, December 23, 2020): www.pewresearch.org/fact-tank/2019/07/12/a-growing-number-of-american-teenagers-particularly-girls-are-facing-depression/

TIP 2: Understand their capacity

4. Quinn, Carrisa, "God Is Like a Nursing Mother" (BibleProject, 2020): bibleproject.com/blog/god-is-like-a-nursing-mother/

5. Barshay, Jill, "Why the Preteen Years Are a Critical Period for Brain Development" in *The Hechinger Report* (October 26, 2020): hechingerreport.org/why-the-preteen-years-are-a-critical-period-for-brain-development/

6. Arain, Mariam, et al, "Maturation of the Adolescent Brain" in *Neuropsychiatric Disease and Treatment* (Dove Medical Press, 2013): www.ncbi.nlm.nih.gov/pmc/articles/PMC3621648/

7. Bryson, Bill, *The Body: A Guide for Occupants* (Anchor Books, 2019).

8. Jensen, Dr Frances E. with Amy Ellis Nutt, *The Teenage Brain* (HarperCollins Publishers, 2016).

9. Jensen, Dr Frances E. with Amy Ellis Nutt, *The Teenage Brain*.

TIP 3: Regard their feelings

10. Newman, Randy, *Bringing the Gospel Home* (Crossway Publishers, 2011).

TIP 4: Cultivate lasting hope

11. Twenge, J. M., Joiner, T. E., Rogers, M. L., and

References

Martin, G. N., "Increases in Depressive Symptoms, Suicide-Related Outcomes, and Suicide Rates among U.S. Adolescents After 2010 and Links to Increased New Media Screen Time" in *Clinical Psychological Science*, Volume 6, Issue 1 (2018), pp. 3–17.

12. Nesi, Jacqueline, "The Impact of Social Media on Youth Mental Health" in *North Carolina Medical Journal* (March 1, 2020): www.ncmedicaljournal. com/content/81/2/116

13. Mir, Elina, et al., "Social Media and Adolescents' and Young Adults' Mental Health" (National Center for Health Research, March 17, 2021): www.center4research.org/social-media-affects-mental-health/

14. Rideout, V., and Robb, M. B., "The Common Sense Census: Media Use by Tweens and Teens" (Common Sense Media, 2019).

15. Rideout, V., and Robb, M. B., "The Common Sense Census: Media Use by Tweens and Teens."

16. Huie, Eliza, *Raising Kids in a Screen-Saturated World* (10Publishing, 2018).

TIP 5: Attend to Yourself

17. Bastiaansen, J. A. C. J., et al., "Evidence for Mirror Systems in Emotions" in *Philosophical Transactions of the Royal Society of London, Series*

B, Biological Sciences (The Royal Society, August 27, 2009): www.ncbi.nlm.nih.gov/pmc/articles/PMC2865077/

18. Bastiaansen, J. A. C. J., et al., "Evidence for Mirror Systems in Emotions."

19. Huie, Eliza, *The Whole Life* (New Growth Press, 2021).

TIP 6: Know when to get help

20. "What Is a Mental Health Crisis and What to Expect When One Occurs" (Association for Children's Mental Health, May 12, 2021): www.acmh-mi.org/get-information/childrens-mental-health-101/expect-child-crisis/mental-health-crisis-expect-one-occurs/

21. Mayfield, Mark, *Help! My Teen Is Self-Injuring* (Focus on the Family, 2020): www.focusonthefamily.com/wp-content/uploads/2020/04/Self-Injury.pdf

Conclusion

22. Powlison, David, *Good and Angry: Redeeming Anger, Irritation, Complaining, and Bitterness* (New Growth Press, 2016).

a division of 10 of those.com

10Publishing is the publishing house of **10ofThose**.
It is committed to producing quality Christian
resources that are biblical and accessible.

www.10ofthose.com is our online retail arm selling
thousands of quality books at discounted prices.

For information contact: **info@10ofthose.com**
or check out our website: **www.10ofthose.com**